St. Pete Blue

Tertium Quid Press
Saint Paul, Minnesota
2015

Tertium Quid Press
St. Paul, Minnesota 55104

ISBN-13: 978-1511628365
ISBN-10: 1511628367

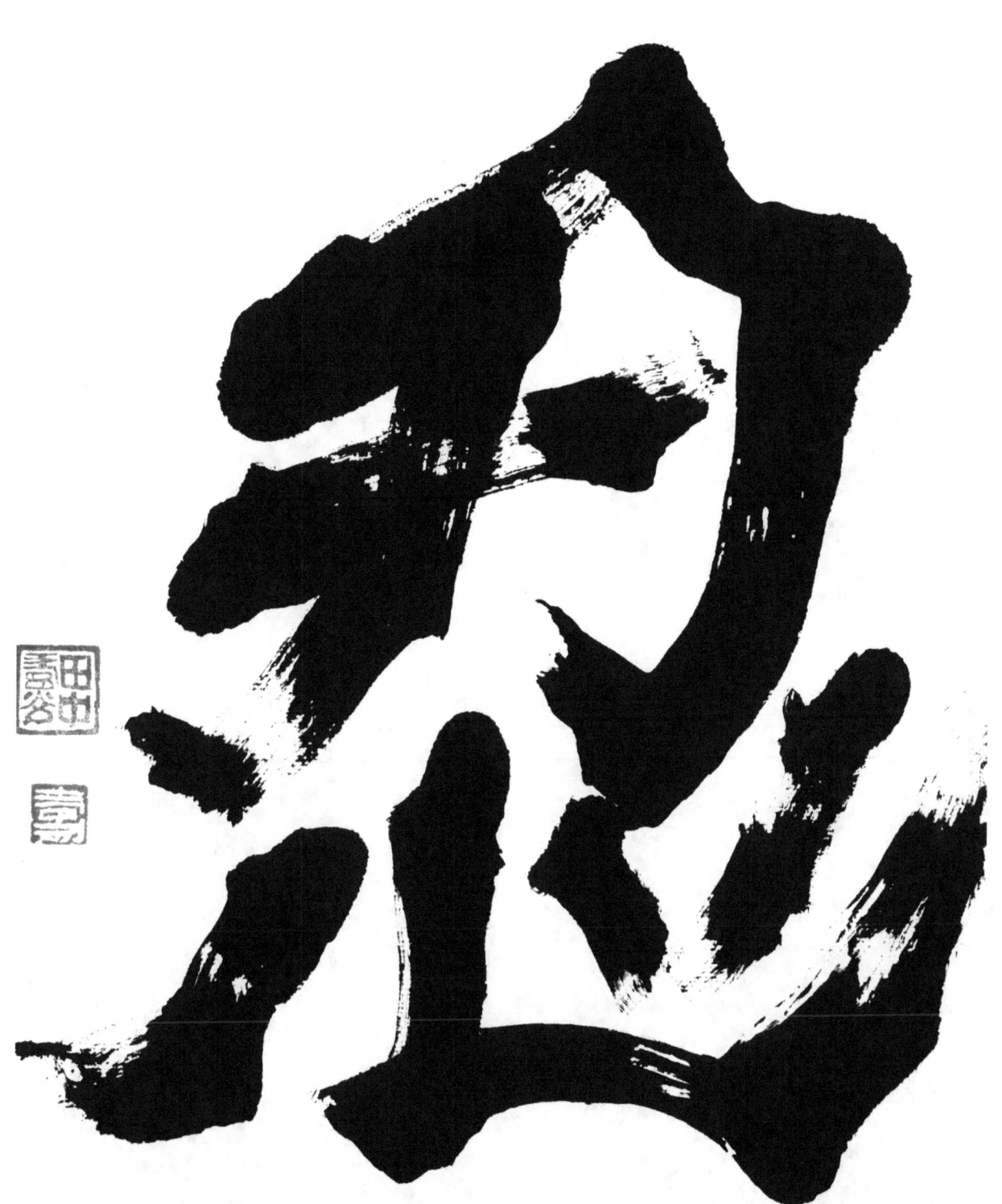

ST. PETE BLUE 1969: A DOSSIER

A dossier (Fluxus Artus) based upon a catalogue compiled of Jack Kerouac's Literary artifacts at the time of his 1969 death, St. Petersburg Florida with selected photographs and texts from **_Logos: A Journal_** (1969) FPC (Eckerd College) St. Petersburg, Florida.

In honor of David Wise and fellow students and teachers at FPC 1969 and Ray Johnson and the student/teacher community at Black Mountain College circa 1949

Constructed by Walter Enloe, Hamline University (an auto-ethnographic dossier)

TERTIUM QUID PRESS
St. Paul, Minnesota
August 9, 2006

Teacher (OE teacon) one who causes others to learn by example or experience

In honor of James Carlson, Teacher, Mentor, Activist
So mindful and soulful an existential ONE; graduating
from Hamline University in 1940, studying with Eric
Bentley, newly arrived from Black Mountain College
to Minnesota; theater guru of religious conscience at
Hamline until he came to FPC (Eckerd) in 1960
Bringing Ionesco and Brecht, theatre of the circle,
In the round, concerning angst and the absurd, awe
And wonder in/of the human and human condition,
And when the college sold its soul to a snake oil salesman
who wanted his own little rotc army, Jim stood up and
fought and won, losing his conscientious post, inspiring his
students to walk their talk.
God's little joy

April 2015

To the Reader:

St. Pete Blue was originally developed in 2005 from "intersecting" materials collected or developed in 1969 in St. Petersburg, Florida while I was a student at Eckerd College ("FPC"). One set of ephemera is from 1968-1969 when I was part of a project team, led by my roommate graphic artist David Wise, to create, develop and publish an *avant garde* yearbook that eventually took the form of loose-leaf, inter-connected papers of photographs and narratives stored in a square, cardboard container. The "idea" for this format derives from our studies with one of our literature professors, Bob Detweiler, of the following artists' works, among others: William Burroughs' *Naked Lunch* (1959), loosely connected vignettes that could be read in any order. Julio Cortazar's *Hopscotch* (1963, 1966) whose chapters could also be read in any order. There was John Barth's postmodern essay, *"The Literature of Exhaustion"* (1967). And his text *Lost in The Funhouse* (1968) which opens with "Frame-Tale," a "story" in which "ONCE UPON A TIME THERE" and "WAS A STORY THAT BEGAN" are printed vertically, one on each side of the paper. It is intended to be cut by the reader and the ends fastened together (after being twisted) into a *Mobius strip* (a loop with no beginning or end). John Cage's experiments with music and experience, and even Kerouac's *Visions of Gerard* (1963) with its existential jazz riffs of illusions and realities, were also influential as we took their ideas to create, to invent, to explore, to experiment seriously with 'text'. The second ephemera set is a "catalogue" of some twenty pages from the fall of 1969 based upon the literary effects of Jack Kerouac found in his bedroom/study following his death, and catalogued by Bob Detweiler with my assistance. Together these materials may form an auto-ethnographic expression of whatever meanings you may make of the semiotic experience here-with-in.

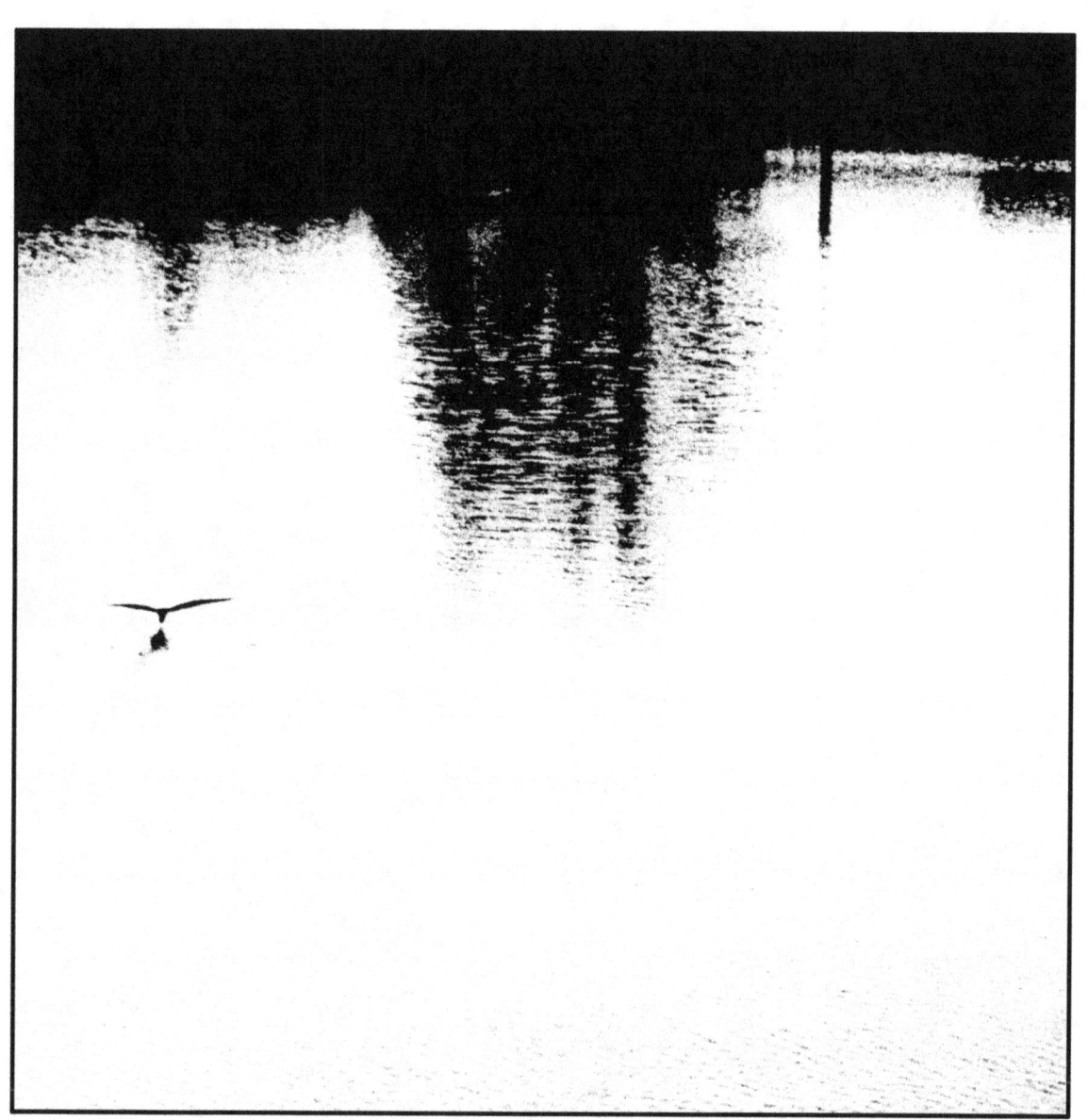

ST. PETE BLUE

a catalogue of jack kerouac's literary artifacts as found in his study at the time of his death
October 21,1969

Compiled by Robert Detweiler and Walter Enloe
Saint Petersburg Florida
November- December, 1969

"I hope it is true that a man can die and yet not only live in others but give them life, and not only life but that great consciousness of life" - Jack Kerouac

I
CORRESPONDENCE FROM GREGORY CORSO

Located in the top drawer of the wooden dresser in Mr. Kerouac's study. The correspondence consists of the following:

twelve letters

six postcards

one birth announcement

II
WORKS COMPOSED ON ROLLS OP TELETYPE PAPER

Not listed in order of composition. These rolls are piled in the bottom drawer of the wooden dresser in Mr. Kerouac's study. (removed front to back, top to bottom)

Beat Spotlight (notes)

Beat Spotlight (unpublished)

Big Sur Pastel Scroll (drawing)

Big Sur

Big Sur rejects

B.T. (false starts)

II (cont.)

Bums rejects

Dharma Bums

God's Wisdom

God's Wisdom (unfitted on roll)

God on the Railroad

Memory Babe (unpublished)

Origins of The Beat Generation

True Magazine reject

Best Traveler, two false starts

Vanity of Duluoz

Vanity, false start

III
SMALL NOTEBOOKS

Most of these are pocket size and contain sketches, notes, poems, etc., many of which serve as the basis for later novels and essays. They are in the bottom drawer of the wooden dresser (along with the Teletype rolls separated by a cardboard partition) in Mr. Kerouac's study and are listed here in the order in which Mr. Kerouac arranged them. According to Mrs. Stella Kerouac this order is important, for it indicated how the author returned to the notebooks for material to include in the fiction and essays he was composing at particular times. The brackets around various listings indicate notebooks held together by rubber bands, and may show that the author used these together as aids for a particular piece of writing. The notebooks are listed according to Mr. Kerouac's designations on the covers or, if such are lacking, according to first titles and headings listed inside the notebooks.

Play, Beat Generation, Acts I and II

(Road 1; Road 2; Road 3)

Mill Calley '56, Notes to Music

New Mexico Blues, Washington D,C. Blues, Poems 1957

WM 1,1953

(1940; 1945; 1947; 1954, Lowell Sketches, Skl3, Mulunka Putta; 1960, rejected Beat Traveller)

III (cont,)

(Dharma A; Dharma 1; Dhanna 2; Dharma
3; Dharma ; 4 Dharma 5; Dharma 6, Ml;
Dharma 7; Dharma 8; Dharma 9; Dharma 10
1948)

Benzedrine Vision, Mexico City 1952

MacDougal Street Blues, '55 Spring

San Fran Blues 1954

Louisiana Traveler fill-ins '60

(Visions of Cody Memorandum Book 1;
Memorandum Book 2; Memorandum Book 3;
Memorandum Book 4; Memorandum Book 5;
Memorandum Book 6; Memorandum Book 7;
Memorandum Book 8)

(Sketches, SK 0"A, Book of Sketches; SKO-B;
SKO-C; SKO-D; SKI; SK 2; SK 3; SK4; SK5; SK6:
SK 7; SK 8; SK 9; OBB, SK 10;SK11)

(Passing Thru 1; Passing Thru 2; Passing
Thru 3 ; Passing Thru 4; Passing Thru 5 ;
Passing Thru 6;. Passing Thru 7;
Passing Thru 8; Passing Thru 9 ;
Passing Thru 10)

(Visions of Gerard Gl; Visions of Gerard G2;;
Visions of Gerard G3; Visions of Gerard G4)

(Dharma 11 1956, Desolation Peak; Feb 57 2;
Feb-May57 3; 1957 4 ; Berk 57 5;
Mexico, Summer 1957 6; Orlando, Autumn
57 Dec;57 8)

(Doctor Sax 1:1 ((Cuadcrno paraToquic-ruphia on
the cover)); 2; 3; 4)

(Book of Dreams 1; Dr 2 and 3; Dr 4; Dr 5;
Dr 6; DR 7; Dr 8; Dr 9; Dr 10; Dr 11; DR 12; Book of
Dreams 13/ 1955; Berkeley Blues, etc.; Dr. 14)

(Daydreams 1; Tics 1)

(Mexico City Blues; MC 1; MC 2; MC 4; MC T2)

1952

Richmond Hall Blues, Sept. 53

Visions of Bill/ Duluoz Legend, personae names

Buddha Tells Us, or, Wake Up (this is a lined
typewriter-size paper folded around a notebook
with Essential Mind on the cover)

III (cont.)

Gnashing Phantoms and Hot Ports
(Desolation Angels Dl D2 D3 D4 D5 D6)

SEA

(Maggie Cassidy Mary II Mary III)

(A 1961; B 1962 ; C ; C 1963 Satori in Paris II,D;
Satori in Paris III,E; F; G)

(1957 Notes, Orlando; 1958,0rlando Blues 1;
Northport, Summer 58; Fall 58;
Winter 1958-59; Spring 59;
Early Summer 59; Late Summer 59)

(Sept 59; Fall 59 to 60 (Jan); Trip Trap,
Nov-Dec 59; Early 1960; Book of Spring
1960; Summer 1960; Big Sur 1960; Fall
1960; Late 1960)

(Winter to Spring ; Orlando 1961; Mexico
1961, First Weeks; Mexico, Last Weeks;
Mexico, Last Day and Orlando, and Orlando,
Late Winter; Orlando, Fall 1961; Late Fall
1961; Early Winter 62; Winter 62; Late
Winter 1962, Feb and March in New York,
then back to Orlando)

Ill (cont.)

(Spring 1962 35/on the back cover: No.
Carolina 1956; October 62 ; Jan-June 1963;
Summer and Fall 1963; Winter 63-64;
Spring 1964: Spring 1964)

(St. Pete 1964; Jan-Feb 65; March 65; Paris ;
65; 1966; 1966; LTte 67; L/Italie; 51;
Green Spiral Notebook, untitled

The Spiral Stenographer's Notebook;
untitled 1969

Joredco Notebook, untitled 1969

Late 68-69

Memo Book, dark green, one entry 1969

IV HARD COVER MANUSCRIPT COLLECTIONS

These are loose leaf typewriter-size sheets held between stiff cardboard covers. The nine books are located on the bottom open shelf of a night stand in Mr. Kerouac's study.

Bodhi (oriental wisdom edited by Kerouac, 127 pp. This collection is in a soft-cover folder

Book of Blues, 161 pp.

Book of Dreams, 293 pp.

Book of Haiku (this consists of haiku by Kerouac on long half-pages paper clipped to the cover of a hard-cover thesis on Kerouac by Granville Hicks Jones

Book of Sketches, 228 pp

Pie, a Novella, 97 pp.

Selected Prose Scraps, 75 pp.

Some of The Dharma, 385 pp.

Wake Up, 120 pp.

LETTERS, NOTES, MS, MS FRAGMENTS, CLIPPINGS, ETC.

These are located in the top drawer of the metal filing cabinet in Mr. Kerouac's study. The are listed here in the order in which they appear in the drawer. All of this material is kept in manila folders. The drawer has divisions labeled respective years in which the materials were composed, or, regarding the letters, has divisions separating the letters alphabetically. The designations Cl, C2, etc. are my own and have no meaning other than to keep the folders (many unlabeled) in order. I have penciled these designations on the outside of all unlabeled folders.

NEWER LETTERS
Cl A Trip on Mescaline. 1959
C2 Notes, Poetry, etc,, 1960
C3 Notes, Poetry, 1961
C4 Manuscripts, wholes and fragments, 1962
C5 Manuscripts, Notes, Xerox ed Notebooks, etc., 1962
Notes on folded (loose) yellow lined paper/63
C6 Various Short MSs, 1964-65

1966-1968(9)
Sax Screenplay
C7 Notes
C8 Letters, Clippings, Poems, etc.
C9 Pie, alternative ending; After Me, The Deluge, 1969
C10 Letters, Notes, etc.. 1969

NEWER LETTERS
LETTERS F-H
LETTERS I-K
LETTERS K-P
LETTERS Q.-U
LETTERS V-Z

STERLING LORD CORRESPONDENCE
LETTERS 58
LETTERS 59
LETTERS 60-61
LETTERS 62-63

STERLING LORD CORRESPONDENCE
LETTERS 64
LETTERS 65
LETTERS 66
LETTERS 67
LETTERS 68

FOUR FOLDERS OF PICTURES AND CLIPPINGS

LETTERS TO AND FROM GINSBERG 1944-65
(Some original, some xerox ed)

LETTERS TO AND FROM GINSBERG &
BURROUGHS (all xerox ed; and original
postcards from Ginsberg and Burroughs)

"CREAM FILE"
letters to and from Corso; Burroughs, Ginsberg
etc.; letters to and from Corso, etc.

C11 Letters, poems, sketches, including
material from Ginsberg, et.al.

Montgomery letters

Holmes letters

Snyder letters

Whalen letters

VI

MANUSCRIPTS, MS FRAGMENTS, SKETCHES, POEMS,LETTERS, ETC.

These are in the second drawer from the top in the metal filing
cabinet in Mr. Kerouac's study. The designations A 1, A2, etc.
are my own, as a means of keeping order and also appear on
otherwise unlabeled folders.
Al Scraps, 1950
A2 Scraps, 1950
A3 Scraps, 1950
Scraps of My Tourian Version, 1951
Original Editor's Typed MS of On The Road,'51
A4 Scraps, 1951
A5 Scraps, 1951

Dr. Sax MS, 1951
Parable of America Novel/History of the Hip
Generation/ Old Bull in The Bowery/ Neal
and Jack tapes, 1952
Cody Deaver (20,000 word uncompleted
novel) 1952
Prose Scraps, 1952
Poems and Sketches, 1953
Scraps, 1953
The Subterraneans (original MS for printer)
1953
the Subs. Typed Manuscript, 1953
A6 1954
Duluoz Legend, Legend of Duluoz, City-City-
City, San Fran Blues, McCarthy Hearing
Notes 1954
Prose and Poetry, 1955
Prose and Poetry, 1956
Letters, Sketches and Poems, 1956
Poems and Sketches, 1957
Dharma Bums MS (with Viking Press
suggested changes) 1957
Beat Generation Play/ Memory, et.al 1958

VII
JOURNALS

These are kept in the back of the second drawer from the top in the metal filing cabinet in Mr. Kerouac's study. They are not listed here in chronological order but in the front to back order in which they appear in the drawer.

Journal (Nov.10,1944, Warren Hall on first inside page)
1949 Journals
1946 Journals
1947 Journals
1945 Journals
John Kerouac, The Long Night of Life (no year given)
French "Old Bull in The Bowery," On The Road
1947-48 Journals
The Blessedness Surely To Be Believed
1949 Journals
Journal 1948 (Journal 1939-40), also
1947
Aug 10, 47
Unmarked, 1944 inside
1955 on back cover
1947-48 Journals
1958 Workbook
1945 Notes / 1,949 Notes
1953 Four Seasons Poem
1944 Book of Symbols

VII (cont.)

Claude Breton (inside first page) 1946 Journals 1946
Journals
1946 Journals
1947 Journals
1942 Growing Pains
1945 Journals
1943 (Joan Adams-Kerouac on cover)
Journal 1949-50 (thick hardcover
journal)
1951 Journals, More Notes

VIII
MANUSCRIPTS. LETTERS, ETC.

These are in the third drawer from the top in the metal filing
cabinet in Mr. Kerouac's study, the designations Bl, B2, etc.
are my own, as a means of keeping order, and also appear on
otherwise unlabeled folders.

Bl 1939
B2 1939
B3 1939
B4 Kerouac-Cassady
B5 Football Novella, other prose pieces
1940
B6 Assorted Prose Pieces 1939
B7 Assorted Prose Pieces 1941
B8 Assorted Prose Pieces 1941
Duluoz Novel 1942

B9 Assorted Prose Pieces 1942
B10 Assorted Prose Pieces 1942
B11 Assorted Prose Pieces 1943
B12 Assorted Prose Pieces including
handwritten Merchant Mariner (novel)
1944
Envelope: 1944 "SclfUltimacy" Period/
Galloway/Michael Daoulaz
B13 Letters and Assorted Prose Pieces
1945
B14 Assorted Prose Pieces
Orpheus Emerged 1945
B15 Letters and Assorted Prose Pieces
1945
B16 Versions of The Town and The City
& Letters, Assorted Fiction 1945
B17 Letters, Sketches, Fiction Scraps 47
The Town and The City (original manu-
 script and other sections 1948
B18 Notes and Scraps 1949
B19 Notes for On The Road & other
sketches 1949
B20 On The Road sketches and chapters

IX
LETTERS, PHOTOS, ETC.

Six folders of fan letters

One folder of old family letters

IX (cont.)

Fourteen folders ofMemere letters '39-'63

One folder of Edie Letters One folder of

Love Letters One folder on Athletics

One folder, nine notebooks, one re-inventory sheet included in childhood papers

one package labeled FAMILY PHOTOS

ST PETE BLUE NOTATIONS

Note on the notations: These notations refer to Jack Kerouac's sense that he "kept the neatest records you ever saw;" his biographer's sense of Jack's care for his manuscripts, files, and books; notes from my journals from 1969 related to Bob Detweiler's compilation ofKerouac materials after his death; and a letter from Bob to me on the Kerouac materials found here.

Notation 1 Excerpts from Kerouac's first biography (1973)

Ann Charters wrote Kerouac's first biography, *Keroiiac: A Biography* (Straight Arrow Books, 1973) and also edited his collection *Scattered Poems* (1971). In Kerouac (p.349 It) she recalls, "The Phoenix Book Shop in New York had begun to issue a series of bibliographies of underground poets starting with Corso, McCIure, and Charles Olson, and I offered to compile on Kerouac. 1 wrote (1966) Memere Kerouac that I was working on Jack's bibliography and asked for their help. Jack wrote back (see next notation) that we could arrange a meeting if I was a scholar and gentlewoman and promised to keep the directions to his house strictly secrete Unwelcome beatniks popping up at midnight looked like ghosts at his mother's door...I hadn't expected the care he'd taken keeping his books and manuscripts together, thinking that with all the moving he'd done in his life there'd be chaos, but Jack always kept his paper, his letters, and books carefully together, the papers and notebooks in his desk drawers, the letters filed neatly in a metal cabinet, the books on a shelf in his mother's room. The collection of his first editions had been in the living room first, then his own bedroom, but they'd been moved out when guests began slipping them into pockets wilhout nsking first."

#Notation 2 Excerpts from a letter from Kerouac to Ann Charters (1966)

August 5,1966

Box 809
Hyannis, Mass.

Dear Dr. Charters,

I'm willing to go through my collection of editions in my house providing only you don't give my home address to anyone or any groups. I'm trying to write in the privacy of my own Thoughts and domicile. Also I think my complete bibliography works comes to a hundred pages or so. 1 think I have here in my study, something like 99.5% information for the entire bibliography. I think the rest I can direct you to. T've kept the neatest records you ever saw.

(Signed Jack)

#Notation 3 Ann Charters ou Jack Kerouac (2001)

"Th;it was a wonderful thing because it turned out he did keep the neatest records. Jack took writing as his mission on earth; that's\ what he did. And if he had a day when the juices weren't flowing- and I mean that quite literally- he would spend time in his study organizing contracts or filing letters of his friends together in chronological order or taking his periodical publications and lining them up on the shelf...actually he had about 97.5%; I had to do some spade work. From "A Life in Letters: Ann Charters on Jack Kerouac," *Poetry Flash Number 288* (September 2001)

#Notation 4 Memory Scraps from Journal 7,1969 (2005)

Finding the Kerouac compilation in 2005 I searched my journals and found the following notations, scraps of memory from 1969 following my trip to Asia.

Dharma Dream kept returning nights in a row outside Nojiri-ko a small village of twenty homes with its wood fueled crematory where last summer I had been imprisoned pone night by merry scary pranksters I had pissed off. [Must have to be that trip to Kyoto fueling the Buddha with a thousand faces I re-found again in st.pete's central park, rows of benches with the nearly dead and never newly weds]

Early st. pete fall *(November I guess])* I ran into Bob one morning over coffee; said he was going tovisit Jack's place to meet his mother and wife and did I want to go; meet me at 6:30. Died in October and left a study full of his life-work stuff. Left practice early to shower and dress up—wear a tie he said. Not much to do about the hair. Took a toke in slaytor's woods meeting the waking walking dead; cool night; had found dhanna bums, in my pocket, a votive; never got on the road off the shelf, but bums went with me from nojiri Tokyo to bangkok changmai and Calcutta- the bums, we're the real deal; I'm really a Buddhist Cliristian at the moment- at least I was catholic Buddha man a minute ago; dead peoples stuff is dead; so were his women, gray dark, quiet, heavy breathing.

Went back to jack's place a Sunday afternoon; they were boxing stuff up; the dead leave more than the living ever knew until it was to store the stuff or sell it off, boxes of notebooks and rolls and dossiers and folders.

I plan to go lightly. **LOGOS.........tertium quid**

#Notation 5 Bob Detweiler's Recollections (2005)

In 2005 after finding this Kerouac compilation document, I retyped it and sent a copy to Bob Detweiler and then to Jerry Nicosia who had written the most extensive biography of Kerouac to date. *Memory Babe: A Cultural Biography of Jack Kerouac.* Jerry called me wanting to see if I had any recollection of Jack's mother's health and mental condition. I told him I was sure I was stoned at the time and could remember little, especially in a court of law. Jerry was involved in a scries of lawsuits over the mulfiniillion dollar Kerouac estate and was convinced that Jack's mother's signature had been forged on his last will and testament on who was to receive what from Jack. So then Jerry traced Bob down (against my wishes) and his lawyers interviewed Bob. Nothing came of it; suit was later dismissed (check out the webpages of St. Petersburg Times for this saga)

March 2005

Dear 'Walter,

I'm overwhelmed! And I just read your notes on Jack Kerouac, which brings a flood of memories hack tome. Thank you! 1 read the Kerouac printing and was reminded of my clays with Stella Kerouac, who was lost in grief at the moment It was a fascinating encounter with literary history. Thank you!

Love,

Bob

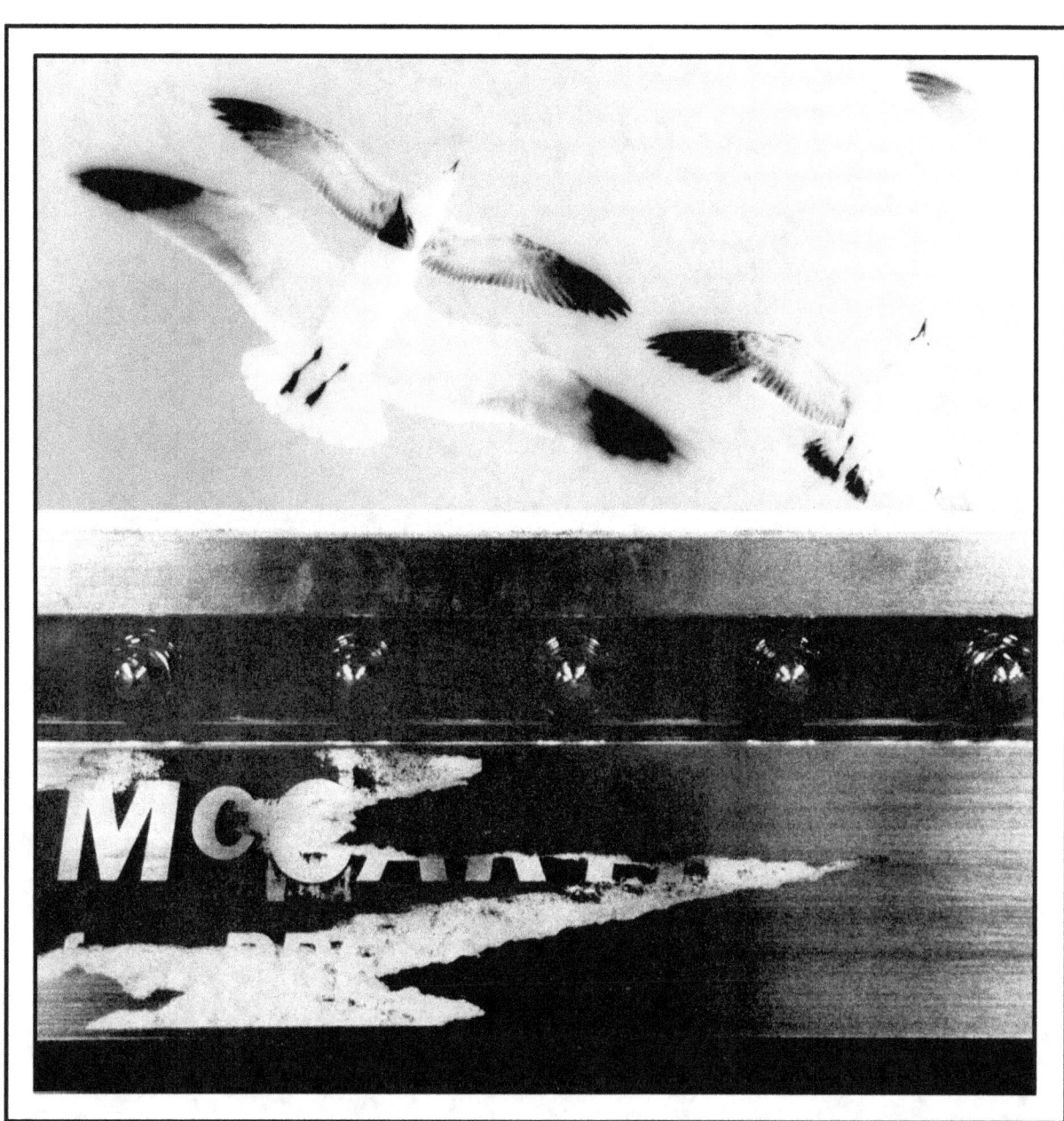

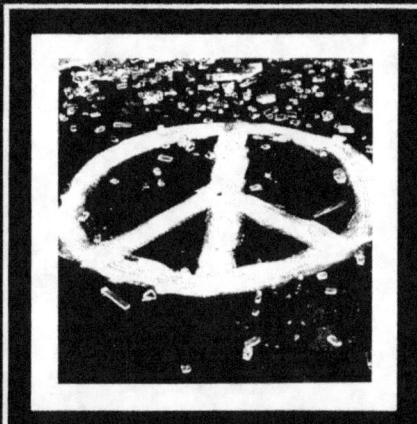

When the McCarthy National Headquarters was raided by the Chicago police, who were, of course, under the dictates of the opposition machinery, a worker in tears asked the officer, "What are the grounds?" The policeman answered: "Coffee grounds." "Democracy is defined as rule by law . . ." (Frankel): Coffee grounds!

J. Nolan

dream #2: I am walking
down the Bolivian Coast
with Che Guevarra.
We are walking up to
our knees in water.
I see myself, very large,
walking along the coast-
line of a huge map of
South America. The sea
is blue, the continent
is green, my shirt is
white. The Revolution-
aries are trying to
reach a certain point
by night fall. We
come across a deserted
building of clean
white brick with
aluminum fixtures and
glass walls. It seems
something of an office
building. We ride up
and down on the eleva-
tors, flash through the
file cabinets
and slide across the
slickly waxed floor.
Suddenly, early in the
morning, men enter
with attache cases,
and I hide under a pale
green metal desk.

                    J. Nolan

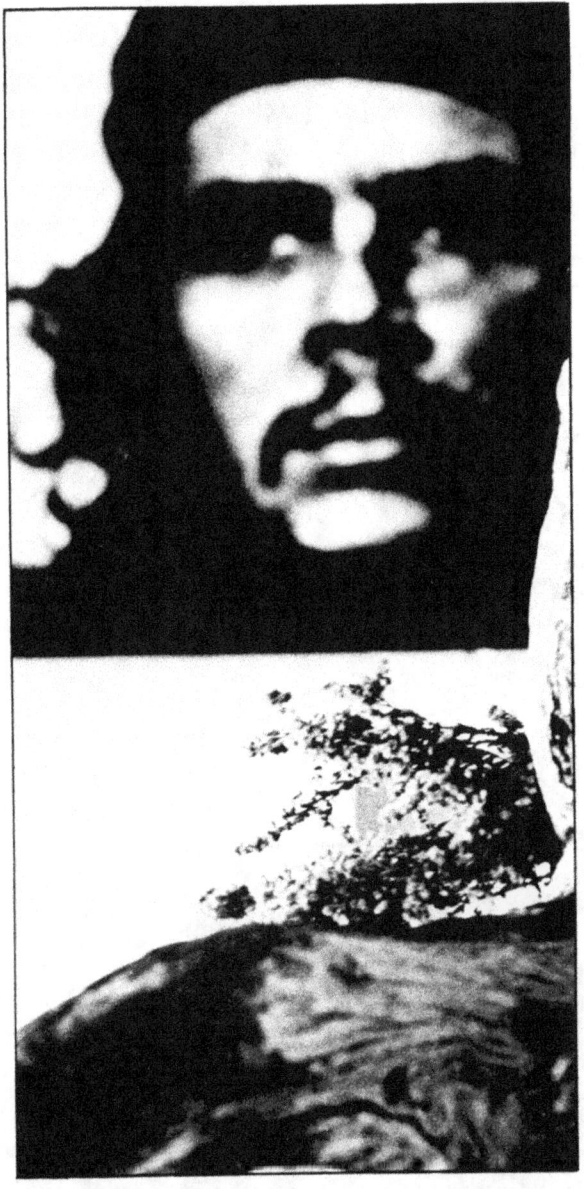

"It
doesn't
make
any
difference
Who
you
vote
for-
the
government
always
gets
in"

Ancient Turkish Proverb

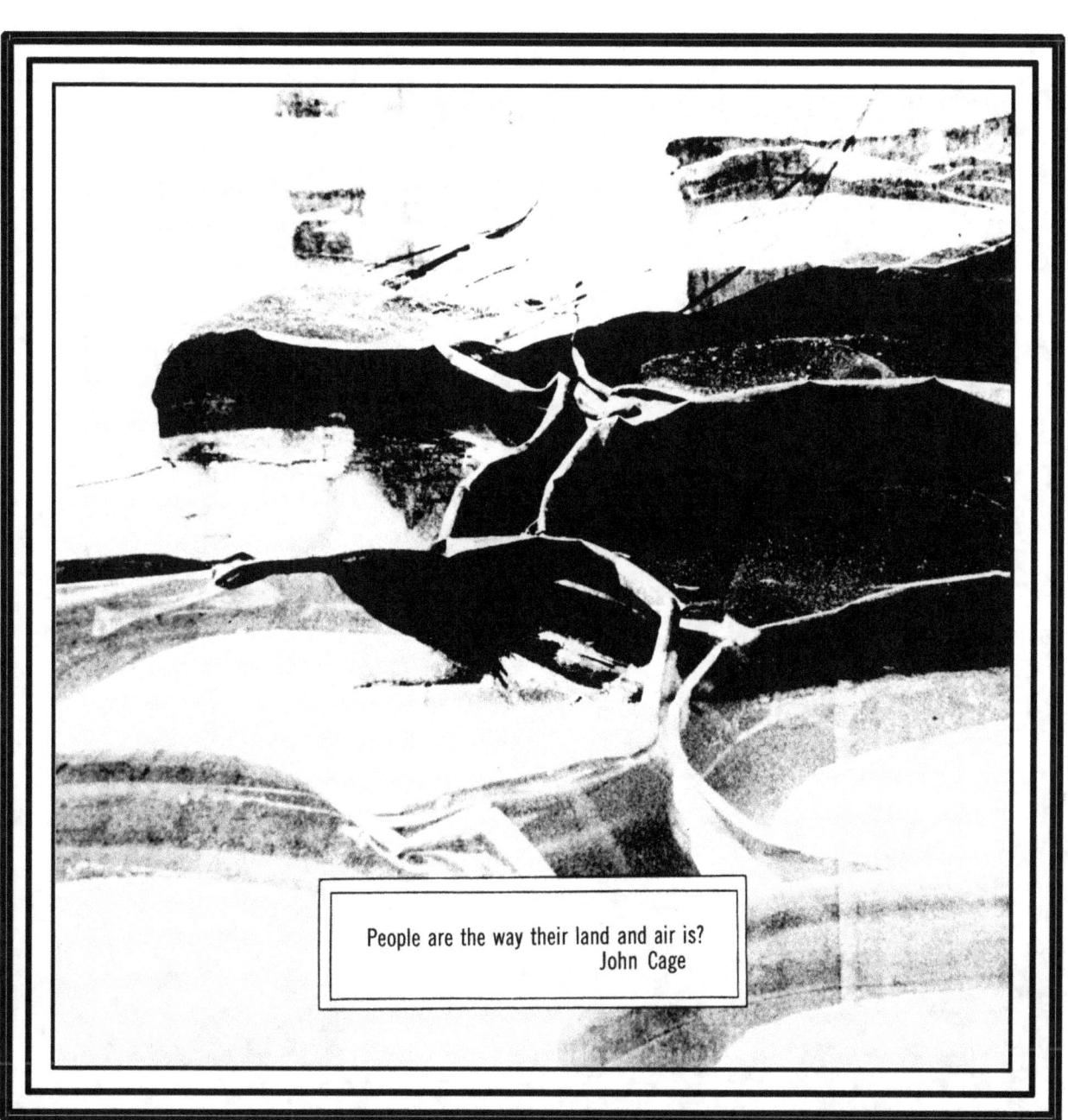

People are the way their land and air is?
John Cage

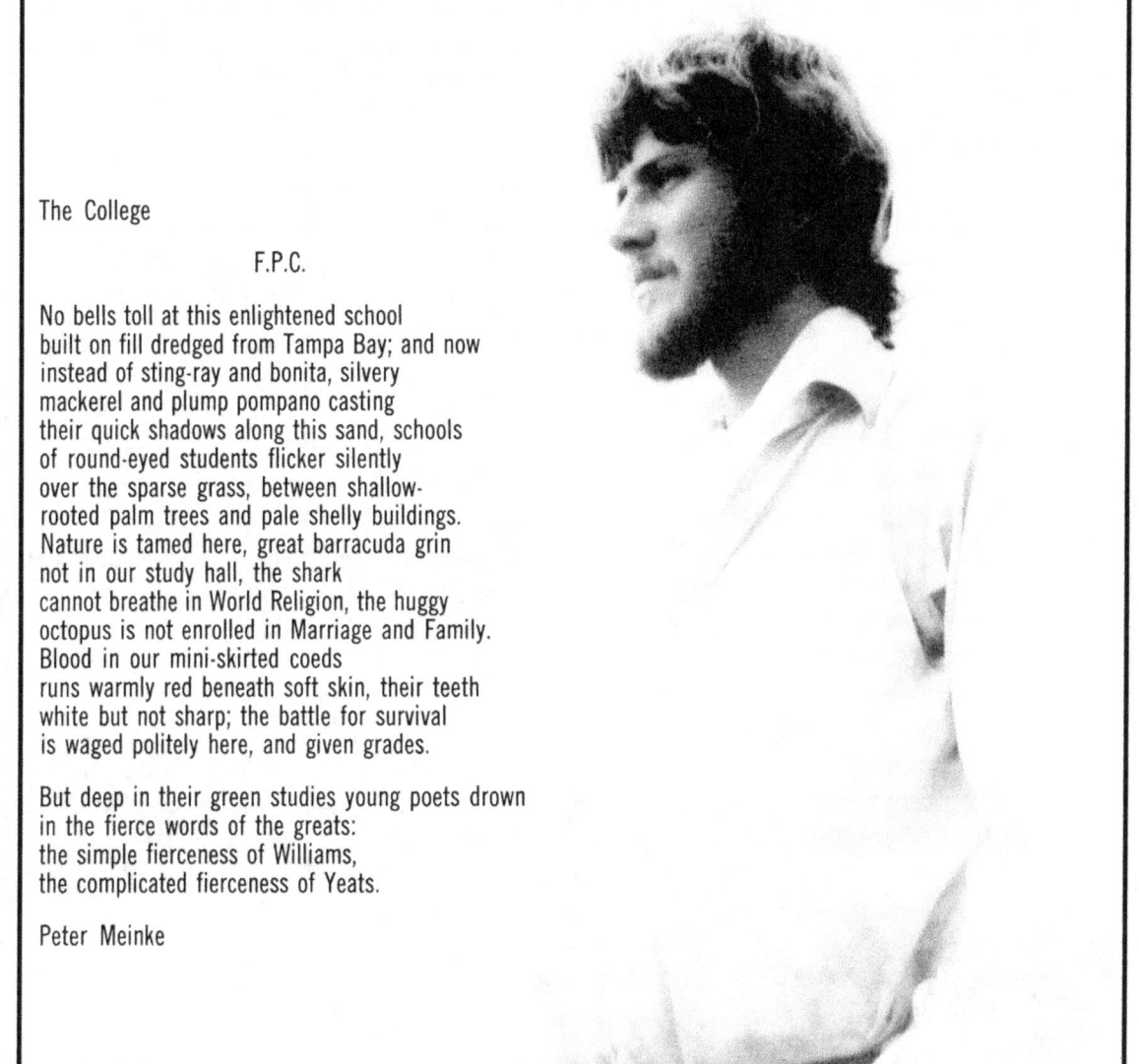

The College

F.P.C.

No bells toll at this enlightened school
built on fill dredged from Tampa Bay; and now
instead of sting-ray and bonita, silvery
mackerel and plump pompano casting
their quick shadows along this sand, schools
of round-eyed students flicker silently
over the sparse grass, between shallow-
rooted palm trees and pale shelly buildings.
Nature is tamed here, great barracuda grin
not in our study hall, the shark
cannot breathe in World Religion, the huggy
octopus is not enrolled in Marriage and Family.
Blood in our mini-skirted coeds
runs warmly red beneath soft skin, their teeth
white but not sharp; the battle for survival
is waged politely here, and given grades.

But deep in their green studies young poets drown
in the fierce words of the greats:
the simple fierceness of Williams,
the complicated fierceness of Yeats.

Peter Meinke

HOWL FOR F.P.C.

I saw the best minds of my generation (pardon me Allen that's your line) shattered, driven to nightmares,

drowned without reason in boredom and mental chaos, thinkers without purpose and actors without meaning,

dishonored saints of the American academy, in their round of pain cast far outside community,

who turned to mechanistic atheism because they thought they had understood anthropology and the teachings of comparative anatomy,

who invented new liberal gospels and theologies and then swallowed twenty sleeping pills in order to free themselves from outworn Calvinism,

who proclaimed the secret apocalypse of Freud as they were dragged off to asylums for incomprehensible poets,

who lost themselves in Jungian mysteries, preferring Joseph Campbell to a balanced bank statement,

who lay in their beds sleepless until three a.m. staring sightlessly into the chasms that moved their bodies and the universe,

who passed their days in sleep because their eyes refused to clear and their reason buried itself in their firehung nights,

who walked down death-lined streets defining Webb's City in St. Petersburg necropolis of the Western world,

who bought the Village Voice in town newsstands while winter visitors gossiped about the hometown news in Toledo,

who smelled St. Petersburg, who lived St. Petersburg, who screaming with frustration swore at their luckless exile in St. Petersburg,

who sat in antiseptic restaurants wailing over present past and future while others fled to New York without giving warning,

leaving behind a sterile colony of inner agony, frozen minds grappling with their alien lives on the barren sandhills of Florida Presbyterian College;

Men lost in the tangle of their web of nerves! destroying the hopeless knot of black reality with solvents of lysergic acid!

Women sinking in alcohol to clamp leaden bars on the gates of memory!

Searching for truth in Zen, Vedanta, Ouspensky, Rudolph Steiner! finding no truth but pain closing in the skull, fingers scratching in the dust outside the gates of Eden.

coming to the terror of kensho at three a.m. in a New York bus station, realizing that self was not self and body was not body,

being raped four hours later by a madman wandering in the bleak morning outside the East Village,

left with scars in body and nervous system, prompting incoherent midnight phone calls to uncomprehending friends,

while others sleepwalked on Pacific beaches, driven to the West by shadows infesting their crystal skulls,

who ran up paradisal hills in San Francisco and fell panting in the wayside chapel of St. Francis,

who walked down Powell Street singing Bob Dylan hymns while the cable cars clattered by filled with gawking tourists,

who prayed in the Oriental tea garden of Golden Gate Park without obesiance to Buddha because of the schedule of the tour bus, who viewed Chinatown in a haze of silk and broken fortune cookies, bowing low to Confucius and the Bank of Canton,

who saw North Beach in a chatter of tongues, Italian beside hipster and topless crowding out the grime of City Lights,

who toured the Haight-Asbury without flowers and wept over sad hippies in the shadows of Grace Cathedral,

who returned at last to their homes, having learned nothing except that the tears that burned their eyes were their own and not another's;

who returned home to receive letters of wordless mysticism from girls who had been granted the vision of belief,

who wept again and wrote mad essays on the East, crying that only intellect could free us from rationality,

who sank into the cages of their own dreams, grasping at making reality from a forest of unsubstantial images,

who stretched to capture their own lost ecstasy with patchwork nets made from forgotten words;

writing under winds from the Gulf, smells of dead fish and cries of gulls,

tearing up sheets of paper and cursing the shredded fragments in a wild paroxysm of hatred for language,

staring at the ceiling for hours on end because thought and anger had both passed out of possibility;

who drank endless beers in endless cafes in a futile effort to silence the voices chanting in their brains,

who wandered through the veils of countless sewage-laden midnights, wearing eyes glassed over and feet turned to tongues of fire,

in search perhaps of a girl with sad and broken eyes, lost now forever in corridors of the rainswept American night, highways unfolding to receive the souls of all those who imprinted knowledge in their nervecells and found too late that the pattern they had woven was the black eternity of Hell.

Jerry Cullum

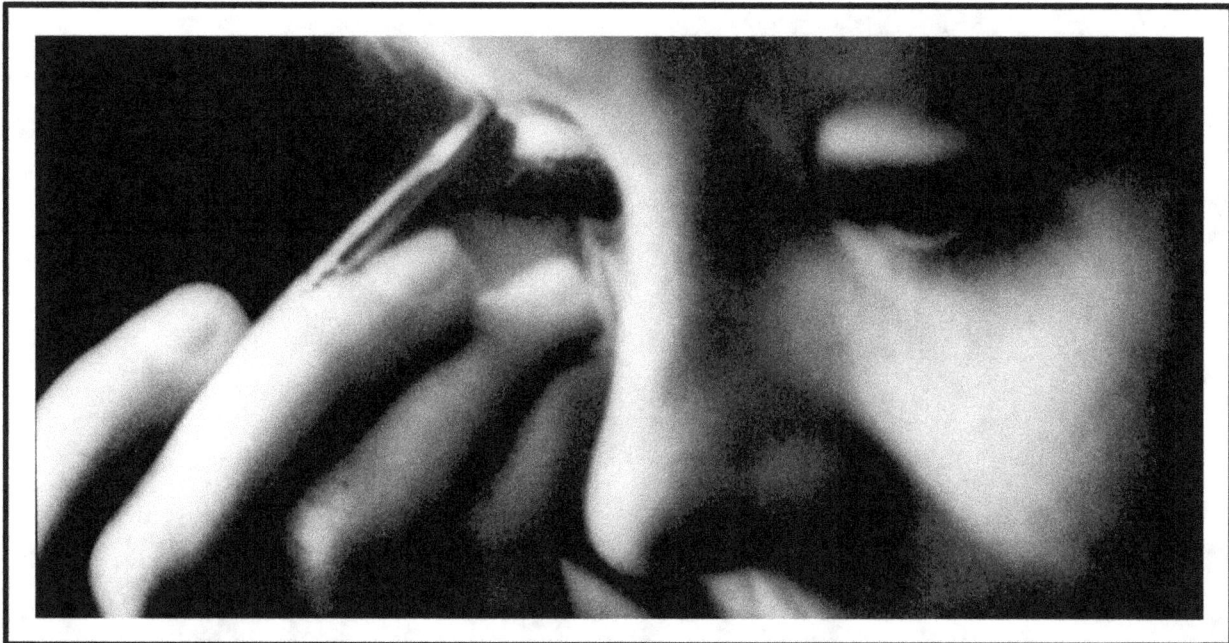

Faithfaithfaithfaithfaithfaithdon'tdie

We all think and feel that we don't know that there is truth to all of this and we-they stand to the rock eating apple pie to the music of "Faith in America" piping from church organs while they die in mind and/or body: all those that you wanted to love you, to teach you, to understand you have gone to the grave, the mental tomb, and you gave nothing and now there is nothing till you find time to place faith in saint francis who once spoke, so i say: help me to understand, not be understood; help me to love, not be loved . . . you must first have the faith before you can keep the faith   babybrotherdaddyenemyfriendfatherhaterhusbandlovermammamothersisterwifeBABY . . .

W. Enloe

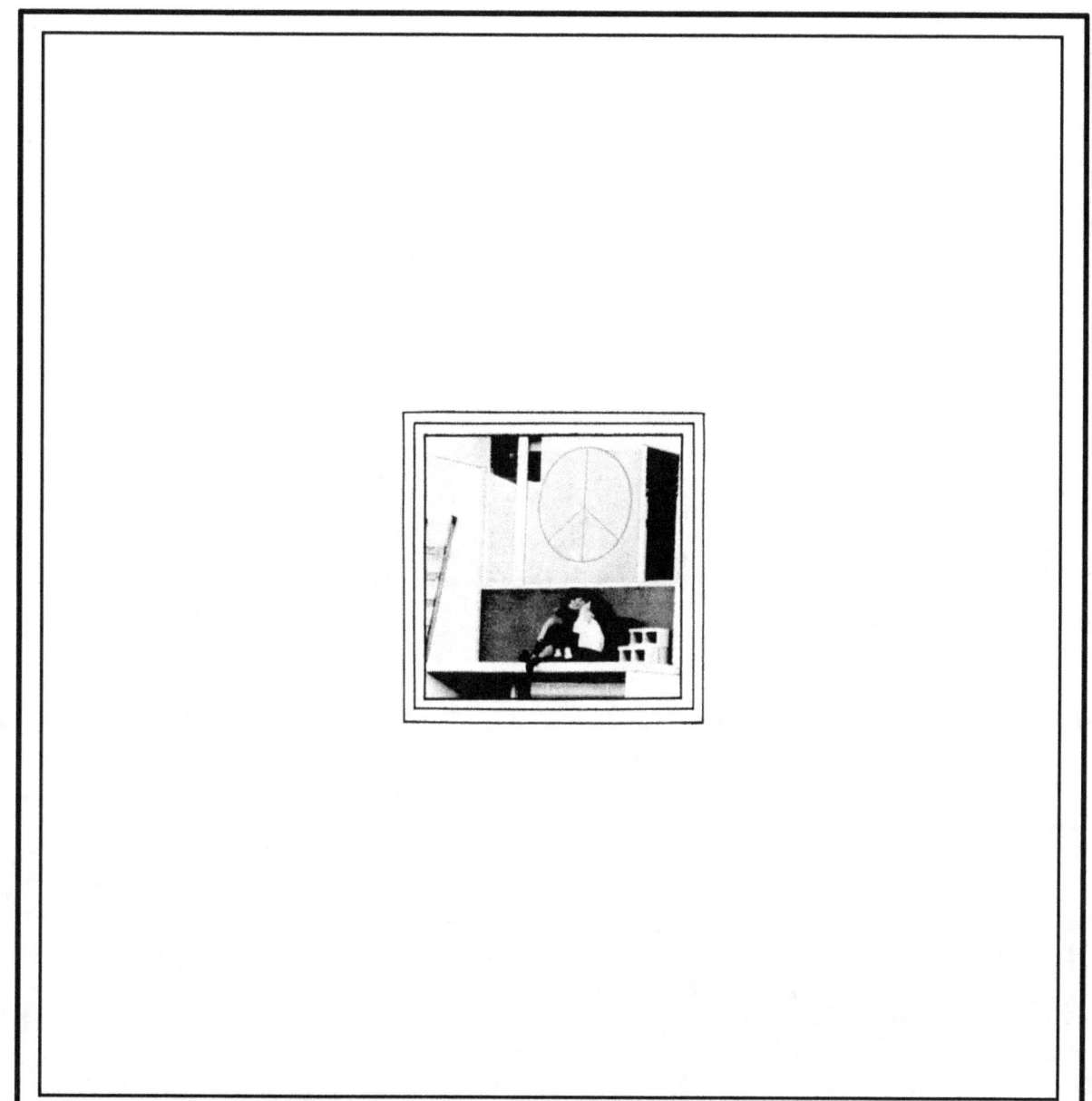

TOUCH

COPY A

LOGOS 1969

COPY B

A JOURNAL

COPY C

EDITOR: David Wise

Staff: Bob Celander, Betsy Dean,

Kinga Dessauer, Walter Enloe,

Peggy Ferm, "Holt" Holthouser,

Claire MacDonald, Jimmy Nolan,

John Rauck, Sylvia Schwintzer,

Patrick Wolfe, Gerry Sandweiss

Heaven's no longer paved with gold.
Heaven's a motel.
John Cage

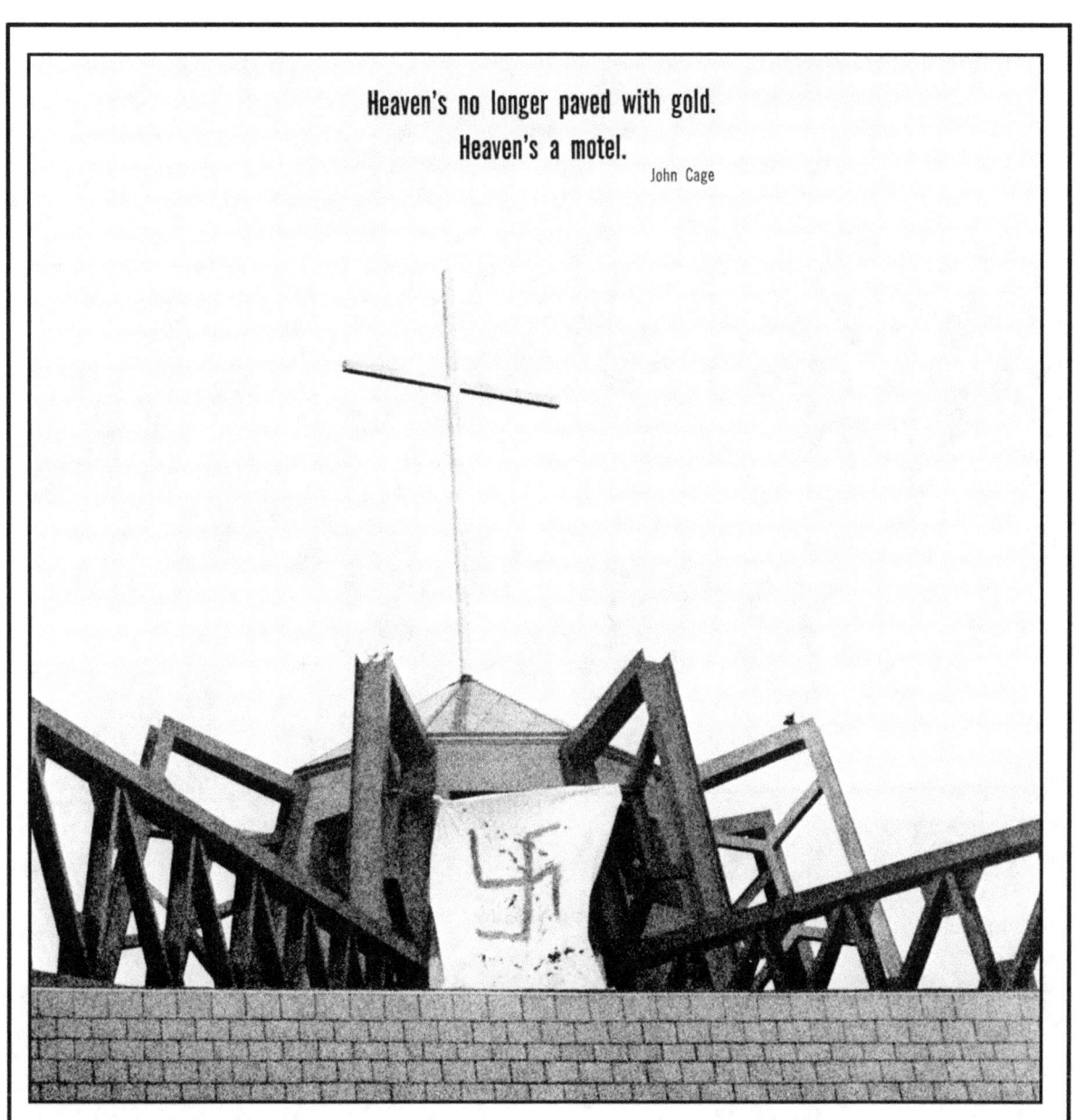

AFTER WORDS 2006

In early 2005, 1 rediscovered a December 1969 manuscript prepared by Bob Detweiler with my assistance for the family of Jack K-erouac. (I had found it several years earlier and misfiled it in one of my file cabinets). In 1969 Robert Detweiler was Professor of Literature and a Jefferson House mentor at Eckerd College (at the time FPC) in St. Petersburg, Florida. At the time I was a junior fellow in this experimental, experiential learning community, Jefferson House, majoring in literary studies and social change. Bob was my faculty mentor. Weeks after Kerouac's death in St. Petersburg, his wife, Stella, approached the college and asked if someone might be interested in cataloguing Mr. Kerouac's literary effects, and Bob invited me to assist him at the Kerouac home at 5155 10th Ave. N. I visited several times. Bob many more.

Earlier that year 1969, a group of us led by genius artist David Wise, had published an award winning college yearbook, a fluxus type object. LOGOS was constructed as unbound inter-layers of pages of varying folds encased in a grey cardboard box, several of whose images are reprinted in this text. Our idea was that each reader was a player of text and that it was likely that "readings" by individuals would lead to the LOGOS' pages taking on different orders and forms. We were greatly influenced by our teachers, literary artists Peter Meinke and Bob Detweiler, the dramatist Jim Carlson, fellow students Harriet Grissom and James Nolan, our visual arts teachers- Peg Rigg, motive magazine, Jim Crane, Bob Hodgell, and students artists led by Dave Wise and listed at the end of this text (Logos 1969 staff). John Cage, Ginsburg, the beat artists of San Francisco, New York, Charles Olson at Black Mountain College, Ray Johnson all imprinted our work

.

In the summer of 1969 after working in an Upward Bound program at St. Leo College in the heat belt of central Florida, I traveled to Japan as Armstrong walked around on the moon. I went to my parents' summer home in Nagano at Lake Nojiri and met up with my roommate Dave Wise who had spent the summer studying arts and crafts in Tokyo. Then on to a mystical and mythical trip to Thailand and India. Robert C. Johnson, literary arts great, a year older than me and dead a year later, had given me two dog-eared, karmic paperbacks. On The Road and Dharma Bums. I discarded On The Road, been there and done that, and feeling I should write my own on the trip I had been on and was about to embark. But I carried the Dharroa Bums with me throughout, a merit badge of rebellion, a votive, and a sweet irony of honor for me, the black sheep, and the prodigal son of loving Presbyterian missionary parents.

When I recollect those years and my fluxus sensibility I find it was not so much my admiration personally for the Beats or the mystical karmic Beatles for that matter- it was our revolt against the authoritarian New Criticism ofadultocentric voices directed at any humanistic form or endeavor, including freedom and active citizenship; at FPC we were intellectually free and yet the women were still locked in

their dorms at ten p.m. It was also my deep felt interests in James' stream of consciousness, lonesco's existential blues, and the projective voice of William Carlos Williams and Charles Olson, of Creeley, Duncan, Denise Levertov. The experimental music of Cage, the kindergarten mind of Klee, playful literary artists like Fowles and Cortazar, mail artist ray Johnson playing reader with text. I didn't know then but my favorite professors/mentors of arts, literature, theater were linked to progressive traditions found at then defunct black mountain college; the small town of black mountain where I spent the summer of 1961 before we moved to Japan at age twelve. In particular Jim Carlson and Peter Meinke. We really were on the road then, finding our voice in textuals and other semiotic forms and symbolic processes; *the fluxus* of mixed media where the medium was message.

In 1970 a year later Bob had moved on to Emory's Graduate Institute of Liberal Arts (ILA) to be Director and professor of interdisciplinary studies. Bob is professor emeritus of Comparative Literature and Theology, and a past president of the American Academy of Religion. In 19711 followed Bob to Emory's ILA to study human sciences and liberal arts. That first year I began to volunteer at the open, progressive Paideia, beginning in the half-day kindergarten, and the time I left in 1980 I was teaching in the high school. One of my high school students Cindy Strickland wanted to do an independent study on the Beat Poets her last semester before heading off to Reed College. I remembered the Kerouac project, contacted Bob who had a single copy of a first draft, which I passed on to her. From Atlanta I returned to Hiroshima to head the international school until 1988; today I am a teacher of education and liberal arts at Hamline University in St Paul where I continue to emphasize interdisciplinary, experiential, creative project learning of which this textual document is a testament. In fact a most recent taproot for this project was at Avalon High School, a liberal arts chartering high school sponsored by Hamline, where the focus is on project based learning. The spring of 2002, the first year of the school, a young woman. Gabby, a self-described "new generation flower child" whose "cool, hip" father was a local physician to fallen rock stars, wanted to do a project on the Beats and Kerouac. I found my copy of that first draft and she got into recreating Kerouac's study as a diorama and thus became another dharma bum on the road to somewhere.

Yesterday my old college friend and artistic mentor and muse, David Wise, passed on to the other side. Another wonderful Dharma Bum he is. With Love. November 29, 2006

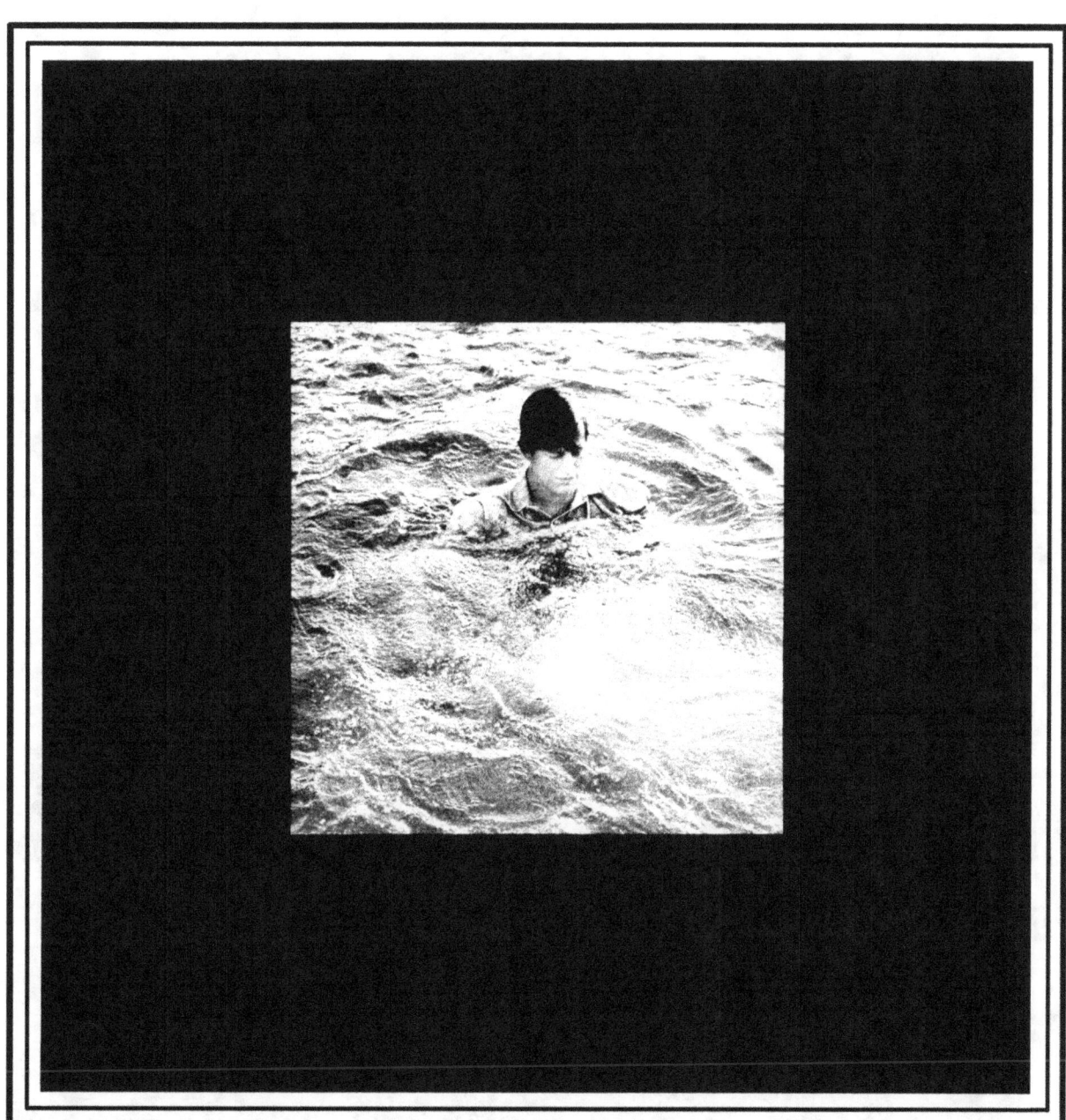

My grandmother was sometimes very deaf and at other times, particularly when someone was talking about her, not deaf at all. One Sunday she was sitting in the living room directly in front of the radio. She had a sermon turned on so loud that it could be heard for blocks around. And yet she was sound asleep and snoring. I tiptoed into the living room, hoping to get a manuscript that was on the piano and to get out again without waking her up. I almost did it. But just as I got to the door, the radio went off and Grandmother spoke sharply: "John, are you ready for the second coming of the lord?"

John Cage

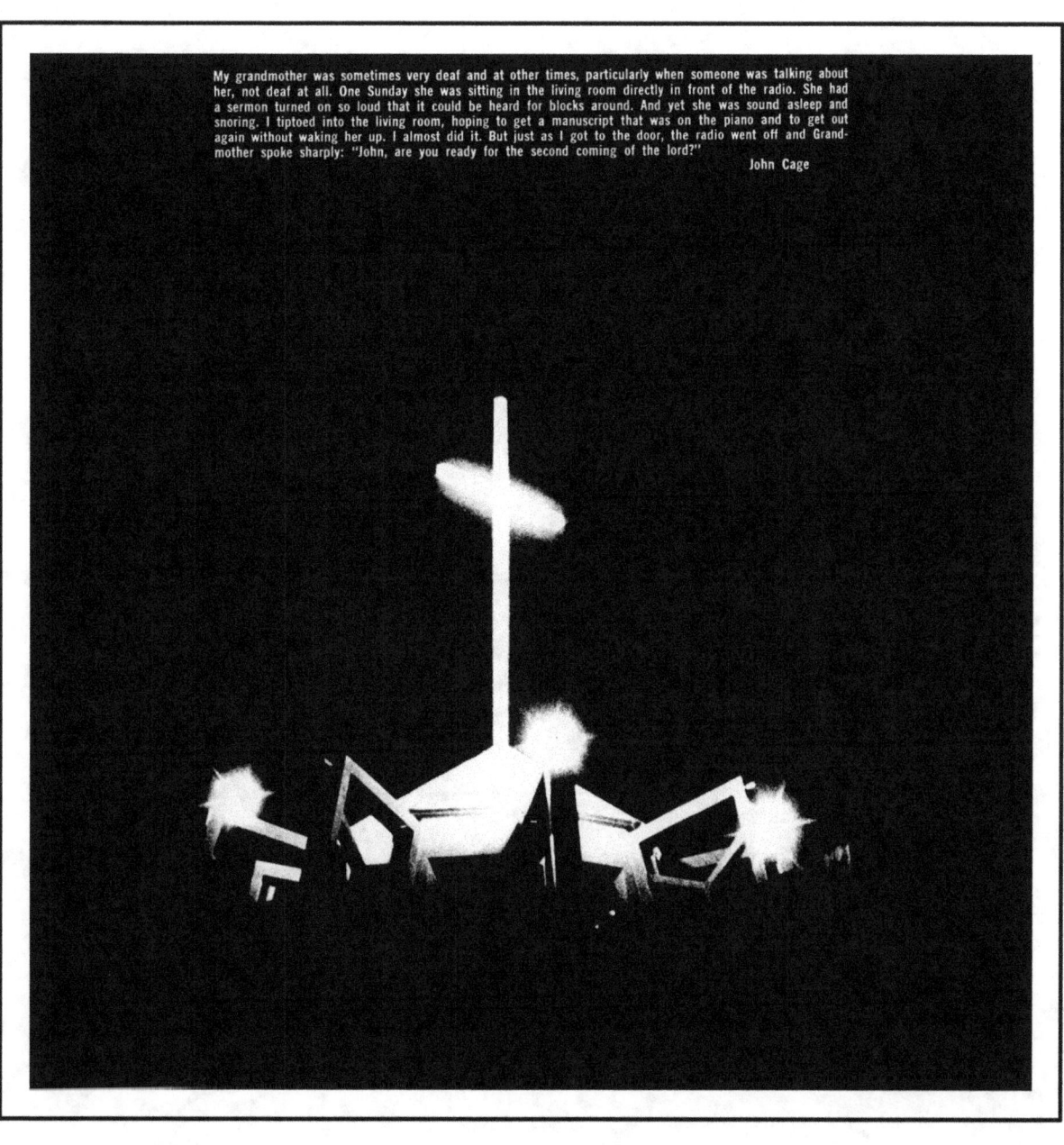

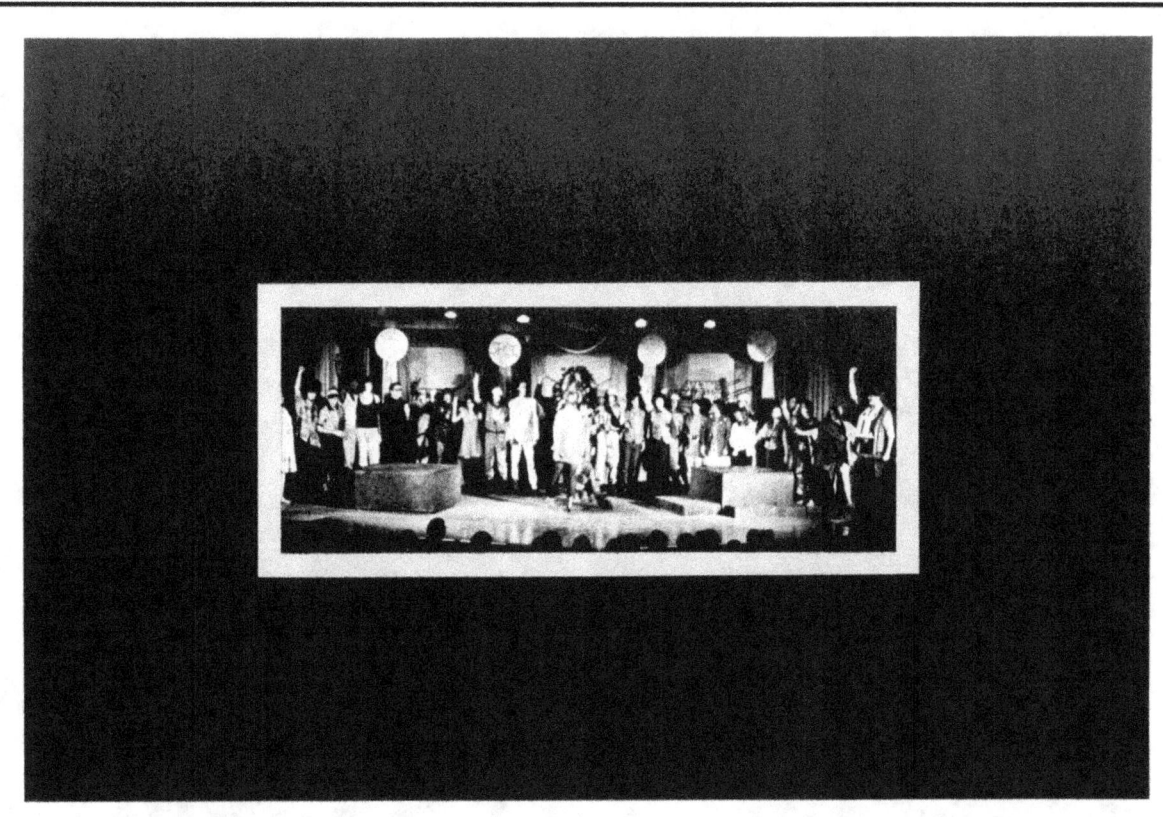

"In America the uniform always finishes first, the production expert second, and Christ was welcome to come in third."

McCarthy to Mailer
Harpers, Nov. '68

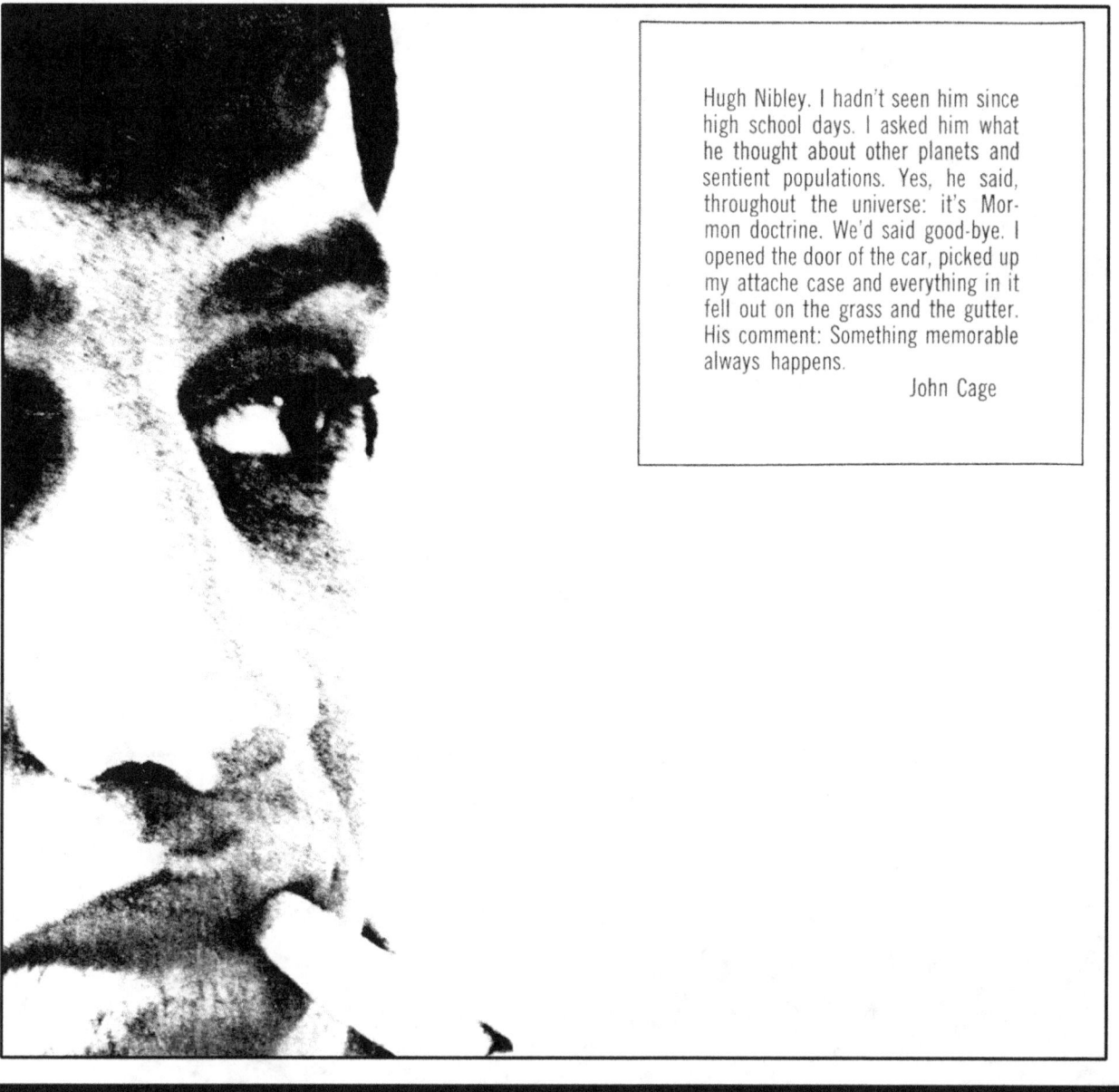

Hugh Nibley. I hadn't seen him since high school days. I asked him what he thought about other planets and sentient populations. Yes, he said, throughout the universe: it's Mormon doctrine. We'd said good-bye. I opened the door of the car, picked up my attache case and everything in it fell out on the grass and the gutter. His comment: Something memorable always happens.

John Cage

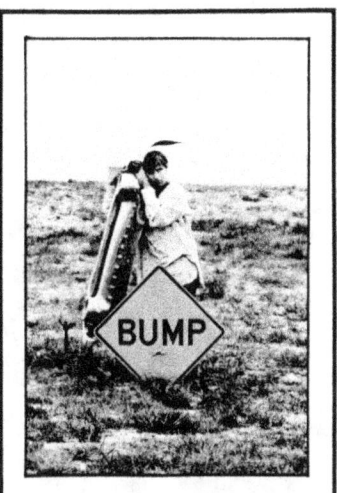

there are three things that keep life
from being so daily
            to make love
                to make believe
                    to make hope
        with
    the ordinary everyday people and stuff
                around us
        Sister Mary Corita

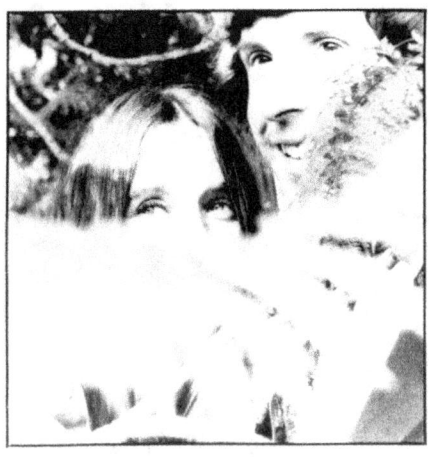

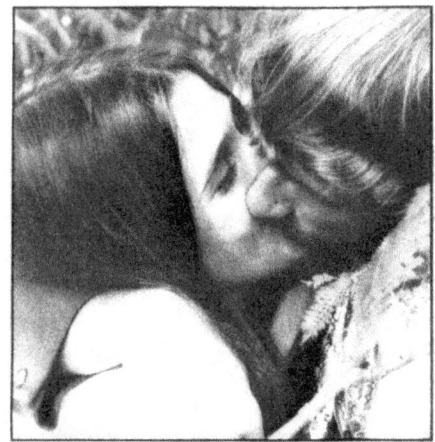

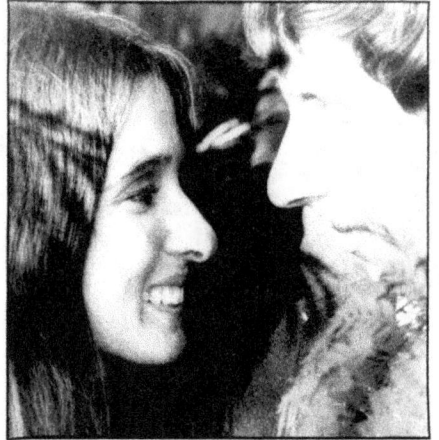

BLACKBIRD SINGING IN THE DEAD OF NIGHT
TAKE THESE BROKEN WINGS AND LEARN TO FLY
ALL YOUR LIFE
YOU WERE ONLY WAITING FOR THIS MOMENT
TO ARISE

Lennon / McCartney

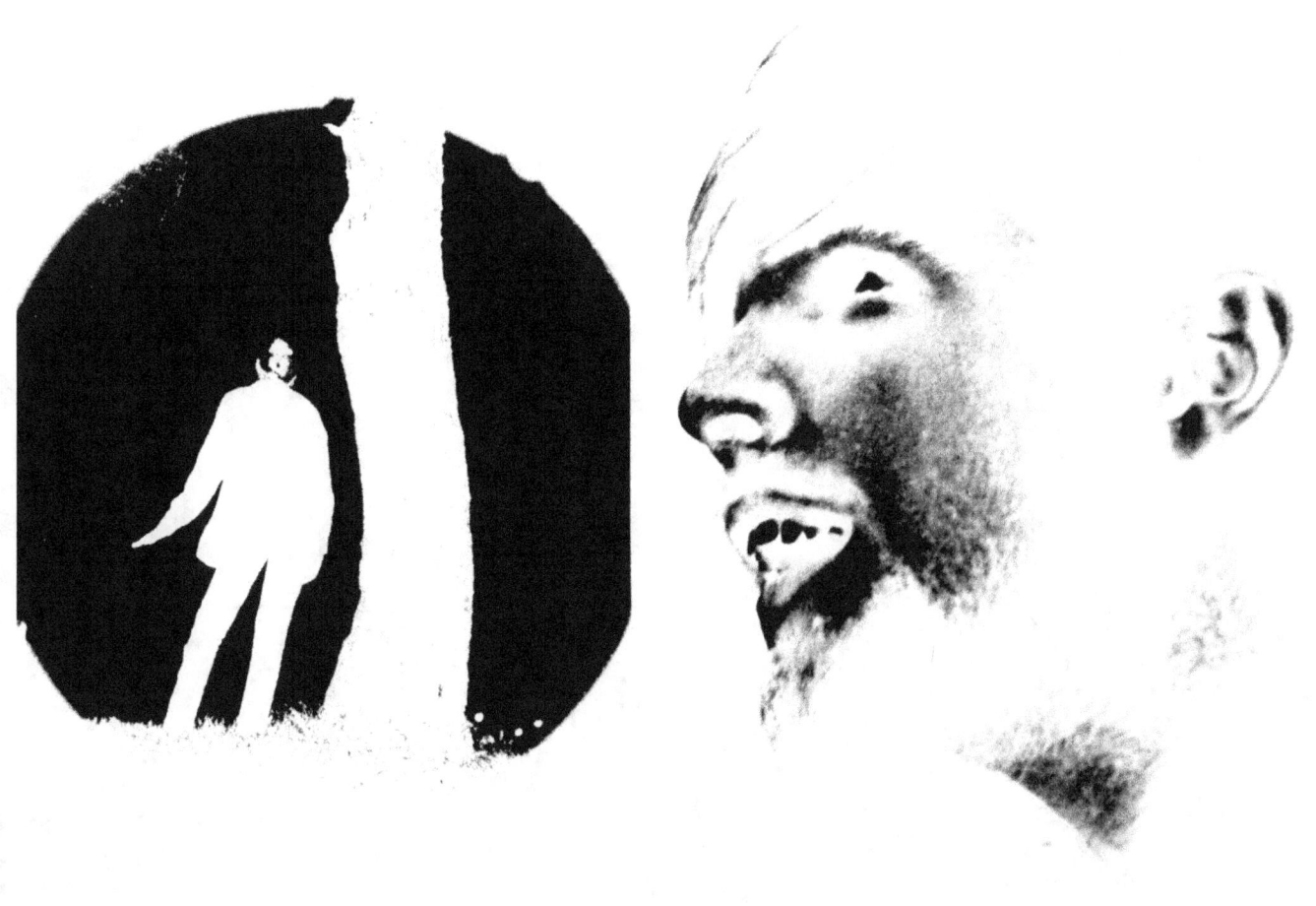

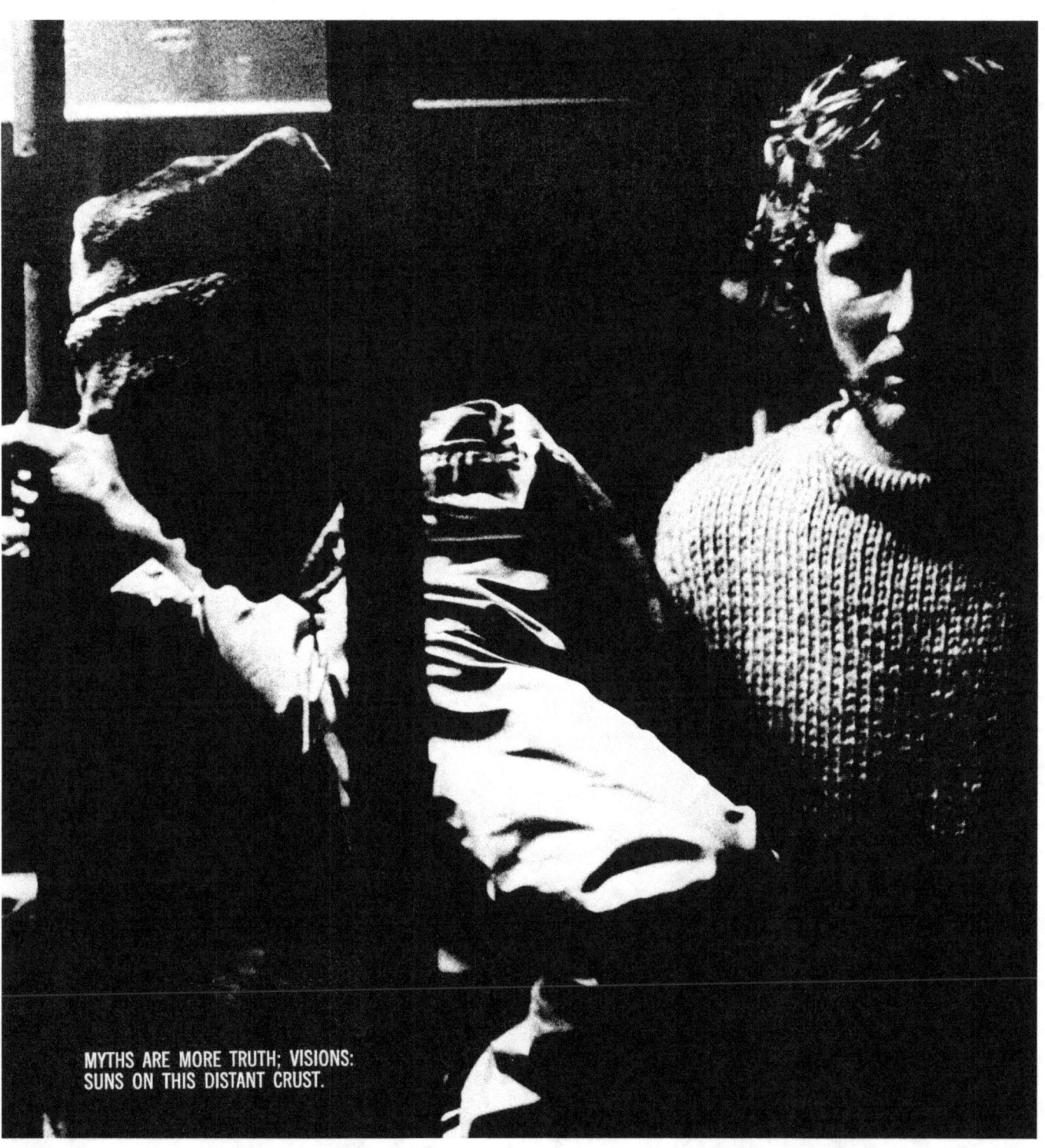

MYTHS ARE MORE TRUTH; VISIONS:
SUNS ON THIS DISTANT CRUST.

ALL
THE
LONELY
PEOPLE
WHERE DO
THEY ALL
COME
FROM

www.ingramcontent.com/pod-product-compliance
Lightning Source LLC
Chambersburg PA
CBHW080828180526
45168CB00006B/2607